AF411622

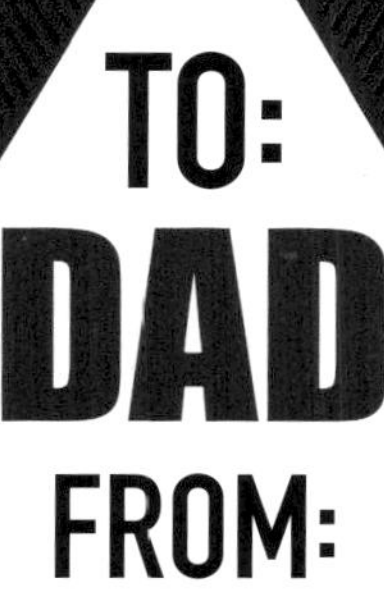
TO:
DAD
FROM:
DATE:

BE

JOSHUA 1:9

STRONG
AND
COURAGEOUS

PROMISES FROM GOD FOR FATHERS

PROMISES FOR MY PROFESSIONAL LIFE

PROMISES OF A NEW LIFE

"BE
JOSHUA 1:9
STRONG
AND
COURAGEOUS.
FOR GOD IS WITH YOU
WHEREVER YOU GO."

PROMISES FOR MY RELATIONSHIP WITH GOD

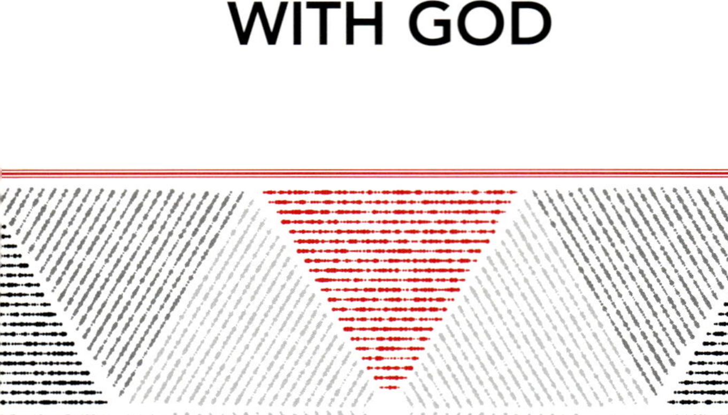

Seek His will in all you do, and
He will show you which path to take.

Proverbs 3:6 NLT

Submit to God. Resist the devil and
he will flee from you. Draw near to God,
and He will draw near to you.

James 4:7-8 NKJV

Seek the LORD your God, and you will
find Him if you seek Him with all your heart
and with all your soul.

Deuteronomy 4:29 NKJV

The Lord says, "I love those who love Me, and
those who seek Me diligently will find Me."

Proverbs 8:17 NKJV

The LORD is with you while you are with Him.
If you seek Him, He will be found by you,
but if you forsake Him, He will forsake you.

2 Chronicles 15:2 NKJV

The lions may grow weak and hungry, but
those who seek the LORD lack no good thing.

Psalm 34:10 NIV

Seek the LORD while you can find Him.
Call on Him now while He is near.

Isaiah 55:6 NLT

"Ask, and it will be given to you;
seek, and you will find; knock, and it will
be opened to you. For everyone who asks
receives, and he who seeks finds, and
to him who knocks it will be opened."

Matthew 7:7-8 NKJV

Let all those who seek You rejoice and be
glad in You; let such as love Your salvation
say continually, "The LORD be magnified!"

Psalm 40:16 NKJV

God
is found by
those who seek
Him with all their heart.

- Samuel Chadwick

Let us draw near with a true heart in
full assurance of faith, having our hearts
sprinkled from an evil conscience and
our bodies washed with pure water.

Hebrews 10:22 NKJV

May He strengthen your hearts so that you
will be blameless and holy in the presence
of our God and Father when our Lord Jesus
comes with all His holy ones.

1 Thessalonians 3:13 NIV

Fix your thoughts on what is true, and
honorable, and right, and pure, and lovely,
and admirable. Think about things that are
excellent and worthy of praise. Then
the God of peace will be with you.

Philippians 4:8-9 NLT

Let us offer through Jesus a continual sacrifice
of praise to God, proclaiming our allegiance
to His name. And don't forget to do good
and to share with those in need. These are
the sacrifices that please God.

Hebrews 13:15-16 NLT

Do not be deceived: God cannot
be mocked. A man reaps what he sows.
Whoever sows to please their flesh,
from the flesh will reap destruction;
whoever sows to please the Spirit,
from the Spirit will reap eternal life.

Galatians 6:7-8 NIV

"Seek the Kingdom of God above all else,
and live righteously, and He will give
you everything you need."

Matthew 6:33 NLT

"For where your treasure is,
there your heart will be also."

Matthew 6:21 NKJV

Jesus replied: "'Love the Lord your God
with all your heart and with all your soul
and with all your mind.'"

Matthew 22:37 NIV

No one
ever lost out
by excessive
devotion to Christ.

- Harry Ironside

Abiding in God

God has given us His Spirit as proof that
we live in Him and He in us.

1 John 4:13 NLT

"If you keep My commandments,
you will abide in My love, just as I have
kept My Father's commandments
and abide in His love."

John 15:10 NKJV

"When I am raised to life again, you will know
that I am in My Father, and you are in Me,
and I am in you. Those who accept My
commandments and obey them are the ones
who love Me. And because they love Me,
My Father will love them. And I will love them
and reveal Myself to each of them. All who
love Me will do what I say. My Father will
love them, and We will come and make
Our home with each of them."

John 14:20-21, 23 NLT

Those who say they live in God should
live their lives as Jesus did.

1 John 2:6 NLT

The one who keeps God's commands lives
in Him, and He in them. And this is how
we know that He lives in us: We know it
by the Spirit He gave us.

1 John 3:24 NIV

"Remain in Me, as I also remain in you.
No branch can bear fruit by itself;
it must remain in the vine. Neither can you
bear fruit unless you remain in Me.
I am the vine; you are the branches. If you
remain in Me and I in you, you will bear much
fruit; apart from Me you can do nothing."

John 15:4-5 NIV

We know that the Son of God has come
and has given us understanding, so that
we may know Him who is true; and we are
in Him who is true, in His Son Jesus Christ.
He is the true God and eternal life.

1 John 5:20 ESV

Everyone who goes on ahead and does not
abide in the teaching of Christ, does not have
God. Whoever abides in the teaching has
both the Father and the Son.

2 John 1:9 ESV

The soul
renounced
shall abide in the
boundlessness of
God's life. This is liberty,
this is prosperity. The more
we lose, the more we gain.

- Watchman Nee

All Scripture is inspired by God and is
useful to teach us what is true and to
make us realize what is wrong in our lives.
It corrects us when we are wrong and
teaches us to do what is right.

2 Timothy 3:16 NLT

Everything that was written in the past
was written to teach us, so that through
the endurance taught in the Scriptures
and the encouragement they
provide we might have hope.

Romans 15:4 NIV

Study this Book of Instruction continually.
Meditate on it day and night so you will
be sure to obey everything written in it.
Only then will you prosper and
succeed in all you do.

Joshua 1:8 NLT

Jesus replied, "Even more blessed
are all who hear the Word of God and
put it into practice."

Luke 11:28 NLT

Sing a new song of praise to Him.
For the Word of the Lᴏʀᴅ holds true,
and we can trust everything He does.

Psalm 33:3-4 ɴʟᴛ

God's way is perfect. All the Lᴏʀᴅ's
promises prove true. He is a shield to
all who look to Him for protection.

Psalm 18:30 ɴʟᴛ

Jesus answered, "It is written: 'Man shall not
live on bread alone, but on every word
that comes from the mouth of God.'"

Matthew 4:4 ɴᴋᴊᴠ

For the Word of God is alive and active.
Sharper than any double-edged sword,
it penetrates even to dividing soul and spirit,
joints and marrow; it judges the thoughts
and attitudes of the heart.

Hebrews 4:12 ɴɪᴠ

"Heaven and earth will pass away, but
My words will never pass away."

Matthew 24:35 ɴɪᴠ

We are
the Bibles the
world is reading;
we are the creeds
the world is needing;
we are the sermons the
world is heeding.

- Billy Graham

When you believed in Christ, He identified you as His own by giving you the Holy Spirit. The Spirit is God's guarantee that He will give us the inheritance He promised and that He has purchased us to be His own people.

Ephesians 1:13-14 NLT

The fruit of the Spirit is love, joy, peace, patience, kindness, goodness, faithfulness, gentleness and self-control.

Galatians 5:22-23 ESV

God's love has been poured out into our hearts through the Holy Spirit, who has been given to us.

Romans 5:5 NIV

"The Advocate, the Holy Spirit, whom the Father will send in My name, will teach you all things and will remind you of everything I have said to you."

John 14:26 NIV

"It is the Spirit who gives life. The words that
I speak to you are spirit, and they are life."

John 6:63 NKJV

"You will receive power when the Holy Spirit
comes upon you. And you will be My wit-
nesses, telling people about Me everywhere."

Acts 1:8 NLT

The Spirit helps us in our weakness.
For we do not know what to pray for as we
ought, but the Spirit Himself intercedes for
us with groanings too deep for words.

Romans 8:26 ESV

We have received, not the spirit of the world,
but the Spirit who is from God, that we
might know the things that have
been freely given to us by God.

1 Corinthians 2:12 NKJV

Those who are controlled by the Holy Spirit
think about things that please the Spirit.
Letting the Spirit control your mind
leads to life and peace.

Romans 8:5-6 NLT

Don't let
obstacles along
the road to eternity
shake your confidence
in God's promise. The
Holy Spirit is God's seal
that you will arrive.

- David Jeremiah

"I am the bread of life. Whoever comes
to Me will never be hungry again. Whoever
believes in Me will never be thirsty."

John 6:35 NLT

"I am the resurrection and the life. Anyone
who believes in Me will live, even after dying.
Everyone who lives in Me and believes
in Me will never ever die."

John 11:25-26 NLT

If we walk in the light as He is in the light,
we have fellowship with one another,
and the blood of Jesus Christ His Son
cleanses us from all sin.

1 John 1:7 NKJV

God has given us eternal life, and this life
is in His Son. He who has the Son has life;
he who does not have the Son of
God does not have life.

1 John 5:11-12 NKJV

"I am the good Shepherd; and I know My
sheep, and am known by My own. As the
Father knows Me, even so I know the Father;
and I lay down My life for the sheep."

John 10:14-15 NKJV

In Christ Jesus you who once were
far away have been brought near
by the blood of Christ.

Ephesians 2:13 NIV

God presented Jesus as the sacrifice for sin.
People are made right with God when they
believe that Jesus sacrificed His life,
shedding His blood.

Romans 3:25 NLT

He is the atoning sacrifice for our sins,
and not only for ours but also for the
sins of the whole world.

1 John 2:2 NIV

"All things have been handed over to Me by
My Father, and no one knows the Son except
the Father, and no one knows the Father
except the Son and anyone to whom
the Son chooses to reveal Him."

Matthew 11:27 ESV

In Christ
the heart of the
Father is revealed,
and higher comfort
there cannot be than to
rest in the Father's bosom.

- Andrew Murray

If we ask anything according to His will, He hears us. And if we know that He hears us in whatever we ask, we know that we have the requests that we have asked of Him.

1 John 5:14-15 NIV

"When you pray, go into your room, close the door and pray to your Father, who is unseen. Then your Father, who sees what is done in secret, will reward you."

Matthew 6:6 NIV

"Call to Me and I will answer you and tell you great and unsearchable things you do not know."

Jeremiah 33:3 NIV

"I am the One who answers your prayers and cares for you. I am like a tree that is always green; all your fruit comes from Me."

Hosea 14:8 NLT

We know that God does not listen to sinners,
but if anyone is a worshiper of God and
does His will, God listens to him.

John 9:31 ESV

Jesus says, "Whatever you ask in My name,
that I will do, that the Father may be
glorified in the Son."

John 14:13 NKJV

The prayer of a righteous person is
powerful and effective.

James 5:16 NIV

The LORD says, "Before they call I will answer;
while they are still speaking I will hear."

Isaiah 65:24 NIV

The eyes of the Lord are on the righteous
and His ears are attentive to their prayer.

1 Peter 3:12 NIV

The LORD is far from the wicked,
but He hears the prayer of the righteous.

Proverbs 15:29 NKJV

To pray
is to mount
on eagle's wings
above the clouds
and get into the clear
heaven where God dwells.

- Charles H. Spurgeon

Since we are receiving a Kingdom
that is unshakable, let us be thankful
and please God by worshiping Him
with holy fear and awe.

Hebrews 12:28 NLT

"Do not worship any other gods or bow
before them or serve them or offer sacrifices
to them. But worship only the LORD. You
must worship only the LORD your God. He
is the one who will rescue you from
all your enemies."

2 Kings 17:35-36, 39 NLT

"The hour is coming, and now is, when
the true worshipers will worship the Father
in spirit and truth; for the Father is
seeking such to worship Him."

John 4:23 NKJV

In view of God's mercy, offer your
bodies as a living sacrifice, holy and
pleasing to God – this is your true
and proper worship.

Romans 12:1 NIV

Shout for joy to the LORD, all the earth.
Worship the LORD with gladness; come
before Him with joyful songs. Know that
the LORD is God. It is He who made us, and
we are His; we are His people, the sheep of
His pasture. Enter His gates with thanksgiving
and His courts with praise; give thanks
to Him and praise His name.

Psalm 100:1-4 NIV

Give thanks to the LORD, for He is good!
His faithful love endures forever.

1 Chronicles 16:34 NLT

Thanks be to God, who in Christ always
leads us in triumphal procession and
through us spreads everywhere the
fragrance of the knowledge of Him.

2 Corinthians 2:14 ESV

"For where two or three are gathered
together in My name, I am there in
the midst of them."

Matthew 18:20 NKJV

Thanks be to God! He gives us the victory
through our Lord Jesus Christ.

1 Corinthians 15:57 NIV

God is
in control,
and therefore
in everything I can
give thanks – not
because of the situation
but because of the One who
directs and rules over it.

- Kay Arthur

PROMISES FOR MY FAMILY LIFE

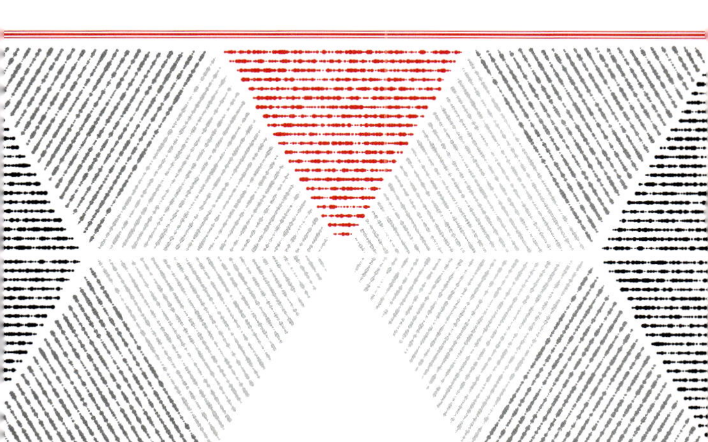

Start children off on the way they should go,
and even when they are old they
will not turn from it.

Proverbs 22:6 NIV

All your children will be taught by the LORD,
and great will be their peace.

Isaiah 54:13 NIV

Children, obey your parents in the LORD,
for this is right.

Ephesians 6:1 NKJV

The righteous man walks in his integrity;
his children are blessed after him.

Proverbs 20:7 NKJV

Discipline your children, and
they will give you peace of mind
and will make your heart glad.

Proverbs 29:17 NLT

Parents are the pride of their children.

Proverbs 17:6 NIV

Children, obey your parents in everything,
for this pleases the Lord.

Colossians 3:20 NIV

Those who spare the rod of discipline
hate their children. Those who love their
children care enough to discipline them.

Proverbs 13:24 NLT

Fathers, do not provoke your children
to anger, but bring them up in the discipline
and instruction of the Lord.

Ephesians 6:4 ESV

"Honor your father and mother.
Then you will live a long, full life in the
land the Lord your God is giving you."

Exodus 20:12 NLT

The believing wife brings holiness to her
marriage, and the believing husband brings
holiness to his marriage. Otherwise,
your children would not be holy,
but now they are holy.

1 Corinthians 7:14 NLT

The best
way for a man
to train up a child
in the way he should go
is to travel that way himself.

Love each other with genuine affection,
and take delight in honoring each other.

Romans 12:10 NLT

A wife of noble character is
her husband's crown.

Proverbs 12:4 NIV

A man will leave his father and mother
and be united to his wife, and the two
will become one flesh.

Ephesians 5:31 NIV

Husbands, live with your wives in an
understanding way, showing honor to the
woman as the weaker vessel, since they
are heirs with you of the grace of life.

1 Peter 3:7 ESV

Beloved, let us love one another, for love
is of God; and everyone who loves is born
of God and knows God.

1 John 4:7 NKJV

Be like-minded, be sympathetic, love one
another, be compassionate and humble.
Do not repay evil with evil or insult with insult.
On the contrary, repay evil with blessing,
because to this you were called so that
you may inherit a blessing.

1 Peter 3:8-9 NIV

Love is patient, love is kind. It does not envy,
it does not boast, it is not proud. It does not
dishonor others, it is not self-seeking, it is not
easily angered, it keeps no record of wrongs.
Love does not delight in evil but rejoices with
the truth. It always protects, always trusts,
always hopes, always perseveres.

1 Corinthians 13:4-7 NIV

Husbands, love your wives, just as Christ
loved the church and gave Himself up for her.
In this same way, husbands ought to love their
wives as their own bodies. He who loves his
wife loves himself.

Ephesians 5:25, 28 NIV

The goal of
every married
couple, indeed,
every Christian home,
should be to make Christ
the Head, the Counselor
and the Guide.

- Paul Sadler

Providing for my family

"Your Father knows the things you have need
of before you ask Him."

Matthew 6:8 NKJV

The LORD will withhold no good thing from
those who do what is right.

Psalm 84:11 NLT

"I will send rain on your land in its season.
I will provide grass in the fields for your cattle,
and you will eat and be satisfied."

Deuteronomy 11:14-15 NIV

God will meet all your needs according
to the riches of His glory in Christ Jesus.

Philippians 4:19 NIV

God will generously provide all you need.
Then you will always have everything you
need and plenty left over to share with others.

2 Corinthians 9:8 NLT

Hope in God, who richly provides us with
everything for our enjoyment.

1 Timothy 6:17 NIV

"Look at the birds. They don't plant or
harvest or store food in barns, for your
heavenly Father feeds them. And aren't you
far more valuable to Him than they are?"

Matthew 6:26 NLT

"Give, and it will be given to you.
A good measure, pressed down, shaken
together and running over, will be poured into
your lap. For with the measure you use,
it will be measured to you."

Luke 6:38 NIV

The Lord of hosts has sworn: "As I have
planned, so shall it be, and as I have
purposed, so shall it stand."

Isaiah 14:24 ESV

Let us not grow weary while doing good,
for in due season we shall reap if
we do not lose heart.

Galatians 6:9 NKJV

"If God cares so wonderfully for wildflowers
that are here today and thrown into the fire
tomorrow, He will certainly care for you."

Matthew 6:30 NLT

Trust God
to provide
all your needs –
He has a never-ending
supply of resources at His
disposal and He loves to share.

The Lord says, "I will not leave you as
orphans; I will come to you."

John 14:18 NIV

"Whoever does the will of God,
he is My brother and sister and mother."

Mark 3:35 ESV

As a father has compassion on his
children, so the LORD has compassion
on those who fear Him.

Psalm 103:13 NIV

What great love the Father has lavished on
us, that we should be called children of God!
And that is what we are!

1 John 3:1 NIV

Jesus and the ones He makes holy have the
same Father. That is why Jesus is not ashamed
to call them His brothers and sisters.

Hebrews 2:11 NLT

For this reason I bow my knees
to the Father of our Lord Jesus Christ,
from whom the whole family in
heaven and on earth is named.

Ephesians 3:14-15 NKJV

"I will be a Father to you, and you will be My
sons and daughters, says the Lord Almighty."

2 Corinthians 6:18 NIV

You are citizens along with all of God's holy
people. You are members of God's family.
Together, we are His house, built on the
foundation of the apostles and the prophets.
And the cornerstone is Christ Jesus Himself.

Ephesians 2:19-20 NLT

God decided in advance to adopt us into His
own family by bringing us to Himself through
Jesus Christ. This is what He wanted to do,
and it gave Him great pleasure.

Ephesians 1:5 NLT

To all who did receive Him, to those who
believed in His name, He gave the right
to become children of God.

John 1:12 NIV

God
bestows His
blessings without
discrimination. The
followers of Jesus are
children of God, and they
should manifest the family
likeness by doing good to all, even
to those who deserve the opposite.

- F. F. Bruce

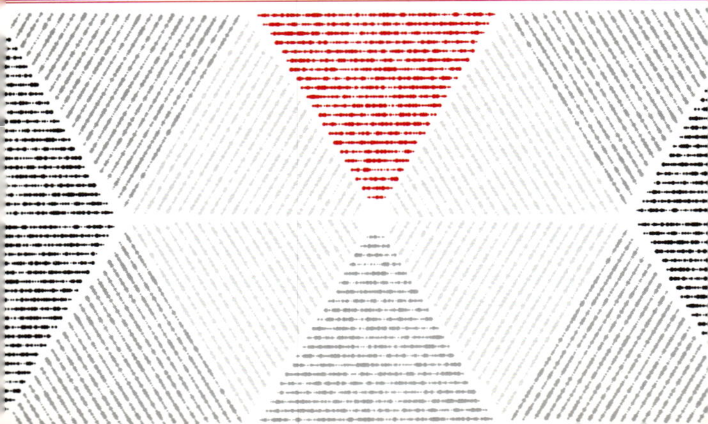

PROMISES FOR MY
EVERYDAY LIFE

The LORD will be your confidence and will
keep your foot from being caught.

Proverbs 3:26 NKJV

This is the confidence we have in
approaching God: that if we ask anything
according to His will, He hears us.

1 John 5:14 NIV

I know that my Redeemer lives, and that
in the end He will stand on the earth.

Job 19:25 NIV

Blessed is the one who trusts in the LORD,
whose confidence is in Him. They will be like
a tree planted by the water. It does not fear
when heat comes; its leaves are always green.

Jeremiah 17:7-8 NIV

You have been my hope, Sovereign LORD,
my confidence since my youth.

Psalm 71:5 NIV

That is why I am suffering as I am. Yet
this is no cause for shame, because
I know whom I have believed, and am con-
vinced that He is able to guard what
I have entrusted to Him until that day.

2 Timothy 1:12 NIV

Though I walk through the valley of
the shadow of death, I will fear no evil;
for You are with me; Your rod and
Your staff, they comfort me.

Psalm 23:4 NKJV

We can confidently say, "The Lord is
my helper; I will not fear; what can
man do to me?"

Hebrews 13:6 ESV

I can do everything through Christ,
who gives me strength.

Philippians 4:13 NLT

I am confident I will see the Lord's goodness.

Psalm 27:13 NLT

Nothing
can be done
without hope
and confidence.

- Helen Keller

Be of good courage, and He shall strengthen
your heart, all you who hope in the LORD.

Psalm 31:24 NKJV

God has not given us a spirit of fear, but of
power and of love and of a sound mind.

2 Timothy 1:7 NKJV

Be strong in the grace that is in Christ Jesus.

2 Timothy 2:1 NIV

Jesus said: "Take courage! It is I.
Don't be afraid."

Matthew 14:27 NIV

With Your help I can advance against a troop;
with my God I can scale any wall.

Psalm 18:29 NIV

"Be strong and courageous. Do not be afraid;
do not be discouraged, for the LORD your God
will be with you wherever you go."

Joshua 1:9 NIV

The LORD is my light and my
salvation – whom shall I fear?
The LORD is the stronghold of my life –
of whom shall I be afraid?

Psalm 27:1 NIV

As soon as I pray, You answer me;
You encourage me by giving me strength.

Psalm 138:3 NLT

He will command His angels concerning you
to guard you in all your ways; they will lift you
up in their hands, so that you will not strike
your foot against a stone.

Psalm 91:11-12 NIV

The LORD your God, the great and
awesome God, is among you.

Deuteronomy 7:21 NKJV

Wait for the LORD; be strong and
take heart and wait for the LORD.

Psalm 27:14 NIV

Courage
is almost
a contradiction
in terms. It means
a strong desire to live
taking the form of a
readiness to die.

- G. K. Chesterton

Endurance race

Let us throw off everything that hinders and
the sin that so easily entangles. And let us run
with perseverance the race marked out for us.

Hebrews 12:1 NIV

"The one who endures to the end
will be saved."

Matthew 24:13 NLT

I press on toward the goal to win the prize for
which God has called me.

Philippians 3:14 NIV

If when you do good and suffer
for it you endure, this is a gracious
thing in the sight of God.

1 Peter 2:20 ESV

Blessed is the one who perseveres
under trial because, having stood the
test, that person will receive the crown
of life that the Lord has promised
to those who love Him.

James 1:12 NIV

Take up your positions; stand firm and see
the deliverance the LORD will give you.

2 Chronicles 20:17 NIV

You need to persevere so that when
you have done the will of God, you will
receive what He has promised.

Hebrews 10:36 NIV

May the God of endurance and
encouragement grant you to live in such
harmony with one another, that together
you may with one voice glorify the God
and Father of our Lord Jesus Christ.

Romans 15:5-6 ESV

We rejoice in our sufferings, knowing
that suffering produces endurance,
and endurance produces character,
and character produces hope.

Romans 5:3-5 ESV

All things
are possible to
him who believes,
more easy to him
who hopes, more still to
him who loves, and most
of all to him who practices and
perseveres in these three virtues.

- Brother Lawrence

It's wonderful to be young! Enjoy every
minute of it. Do everything you want to do;
take it all in. But remember that you must give
an account to God for everything you do.

Ecclesiastes 11:9 NLT

This is God, our God forever and ever;
He will be our guide.

Psalm 48:14 NKJV

Wisdom will enter your heart,
and knowledge will fill you with joy.
Wise choices will watch over you.
Understanding will keep you safe.

Proverbs 2:10-11 NLT

Commit to the LORD whatever you do,
and He will establish your plans.

Proverbs 16:3 NIV

Let the Holy Spirit guide your lives. Then you
won't be doing what your sinful nature craves.

Galatians 5:16 NLT

It is good for me to draw near to God;
I have put my trust in the Lord God,
that I may declare all Your works.

Psalm 73:28 NKJV

You will light my lamp; the Lord my God
will enlighten my darkness.

Psalm 18:28 NKJV

Lord, I have come to You for protection;
don't let me be disgraced.

Psalm 71:1 NLT

If any of you lacks wisdom,
let him ask of God, who gives
to all liberally and without reproach,
and it will be given to him.

James 1:5 NLT

Wise choices will watch over you.
Understanding will keep you safe.

Proverbs 2:11 NLT

God always
gives His best
to those who leave
the choice with Him.

- Jim Elliot

Faith is the assurance of things hoped for,
the conviction of things not seen.

Hebrews 11:1 ESV

Since we have been justified by faith,
we have peace with God through
our Lord Jesus Christ.

Romans 5:1 NIV

"I tell you the truth, those who listen
to My message and believe in God
who sent Me have eternal life."

John 5:24 NLT

If we are faithful to the end, trusting God just
as firmly as when we first believed, we will
share in all that belongs to Christ.

Hebrews 3:14 NLT

We live by faith, not by sight.

2 Corinthians 5:7 NIV

"Truly, I say to you, if you have
faith like a grain of mustard seed,
you will say to this mountain,
'Move from here to there,'
and it will move, and nothing will
be impossible for you."

Matthew 17:20 ESV

"Whoever believes in Me, believes
not in Me but in Him who sent Me.
And whoever sees Me sees Him who
sent Me. I have come into the world
as light, so that whoever believes
in Me may not remain in darkness."

John 12:44-46 ESV

We fix our eyes not on what is seen,
but on what is unseen, since what is seen is
temporary, but what is unseen is eternal.

2 Corinthians 4:18 NIV

"Truly I tell you, if anyone says to this
mountain, 'Go, throw yourself into the
sea,' and does not doubt in their heart
but believes that what they say will
happen, it will be done for them."

Mark 11:22-23 NIV

Faith expects
from God
what is beyond
all expectation.

- Andrew Murray

"If you forgive those who sin against you, your heavenly Father will forgive you."

Matthew 6:14 NLT

"Come now, let us settle the matter," says the LORD. "Though your sins are like scarlet, they shall be as white as snow; though they are red as crimson, they shall be like wool."

Isaiah 1:18 NIV

The Lord our God is merciful and forgiving.

Daniel 9:9 NIV

If we confess our sins, He is faithful and just to forgive us our sins and to cleanse us from all unrighteousness.

1 John 1:9 NKJV

As far as the east is from the west, so far has He removed our transgressions from us.

Psalm 103:12 NKJV

"Be merciful. Judge not, and you shall
not be judged. Condemn not, and you
shall not be condemned. Forgive,
and you will be forgiven."

Luke 6:36-37 NKJV

"Whenever you stand praying, if you have
anything against anyone, forgive him,
that your Father in heaven may also
forgive you your trespasses."

Mark 11:25 NKJV

God has delivered us from the domain of
darkness and transferred us to the kingdom
of His beloved Son, in whom we have
redemption, the forgiveness of sins.

Colossians 1:13-14 ESV

"If My people who are called by My name
will humble themselves, and pray and
seek My face, and turn from their wicked
ways, then I will hear from heaven, and will
forgive their sin and heal their land."

2 Chronicles 7:14 NKJV

He that
cannot forgive
others breaks the
bridge over which he
must pass himself; for every
man has need to be forgiven.

- Thomas Fuller

Many are the plans in the mind of a man, but
it is the purpose of the Lord that will stand.

Proverbs 19:21 ESV

"Do not worry about tomorrow,
for tomorrow will worry about itself.
Each day has enough trouble of its own."

Matthew 6:34 NIV

All the days ordained for me were written in
Your book before one of them came to be.

Psalm 139:16 NIV

No eye has seen, no ear has heard,
and no mind has imagined what God
has prepared for those who love Him.

1 Corinthians 2:9 NLT

"The Lord your God will personally
go ahead of you. He will neither
fail you nor abandon you."

Deuteronomy 31:6 NLT

"I know the thoughts that I think toward you,"
says the LORD, "thoughts of peace and not of
evil, to give you a future and a hope."

Jeremiah 29:11 NKJV

Teach me Your way, O LORD,
that I may walk in Your truth.

Psalm 86:11 ESV

The LORD will fulfill His purpose for me; Your
steadfast love, O LORD, endures forever.

Psalm 138:8 ESV

O LORD, You have searched me and known
me! You know when I sit down and when
I rise up; You discern my thoughts from afar.
You search out my path and my lying down
and are acquainted with all my ways.

Psalm 139:1-3 ESV

"If God cares so wonderfully for flowers
that are here today and thrown into the fire
tomorrow, He will certainly care for you."

Luke 12:28 NLT

Never be
afraid to trust
an unknown future
to a known God.

- Corrie ten Boom

I lift up my eyes to the hills. From where does my help come? My help comes from the LORD, who made heaven and earth.

Psalm 121:1-2 ESV

God is our refuge and strength, always ready to help in times of trouble.

Psalm 46:1 NLT

The LORD is my strength and shield. I trust Him with all my heart. He helps me, and my heart is filled with joy.

Psalm 28:7 NLT

You will call, and the LORD will answer; you will cry for help, and He will say: Here am I.

Isaiah 58:9 NIV

Let us come boldly to the throne of our gracious God. There we will receive His mercy, and we will find grace to help us when we need it most.

Hebrews 4:16 NLT

The Lord is with me; He is my helper.
I look in triumph on my enemies.

Psalm 118:7 NIV

God is my helper.
The Lord keeps me alive!

Psalm 54:4 NLT

Our help is from the Lord,
who made heaven and earth.

Psalm 124:8 NLT

The Lord hears His people when they
call to Him for help. He rescues them
from all their troubles.

Psalm 34:17 NLT

God will rescue the poor when they
cry to Him; He will help the oppressed,
who have no one to defend them.

Psalm 72:12 NLT

Help thyself,
and God
will help thee.

- George Herbert

Humble yourselves, therefore, under the mighty hand of God so that at the proper time He may exalt you.

1 Peter 5:6 ESV

"Blessed are the meek, for they will inherit the earth."

Matthew 5:5 NIV

The reward for humility and fear of the LORD is riches and honor and life.

Proverbs 22:4 ESV

The LORD leads the humble in what is right, and teaches the humble His way.

Psalm 25:9 ESV

The LORD sustains the humble but casts the wicked to the ground.

Psalm 147:6 NIV

The LORD takes delight in His people; He crowns the humble with victory.

Psalm 149:4 NIV

"Everyone who exalts himself will be humbled, and he who humbles himself will be exalted."

Luke 14:11 ESV

The humble will see their God at work and be glad. Let all who seek God's help be encouraged.

Psalm 69:32 NLT

Humble yourselves before the Lord, and He will lift you up in honor.

James 4:10 NLT

A man's pride will bring him low, but the humble in spirit will retain honor.

Proverbs 29:23 NKJV

As the Scriptures say, "God opposes the proud but gives grace to the humble."

James 4:6 NLT

If you plan
to build a tall
house of virtues,
you must first lay deep
foundations of humility.

- St. Augustine

Joyful are people of integrity, who
follow the instructions of the LORD.
Joyful are those who obey His laws and
search for Him with all their hearts.

Psalm 119:1-2 NLT

May integrity and honesty protect me,
for I put my hope in You.

Psalm 25:21 NLT

The integrity of the upright will guide them,
but the perversity of the unfaithful
will destroy them.

Proverbs 11:3 NKJV

You uphold me in my integrity, and set me
before Your face forever.

Psalm 41:12 NKJV

The righteous hate what is false, but the
wickedness bring shame on themselves. Righteousness guards the person of integrity.

Proverbs 13:5-6 NIV

The Lord grants a treasure of common
sense to the honest. He is a shield to
those who walk with integrity.

Proverbs 2:7 NLT

I know, my God, that You test the heart and
are pleased with integrity. All these things
I have given willingly and with honest intent.

1 Chronicles 29:17 NIV

The godly walk with integrity; blessed are
their children who follow them.

Proverbs 20:7 NLT

Whoever walks in integrity walks
securely, but whoever takes crooked
paths will be found out.

Proverbs 10:9 NIV

"Stand firm, and you will win life."

Luke 21:19 NIV

May God Himself, the God of peace, sanctify
you through and through. May your whole
spirit, soul and body be kept blameless at
the coming of our Lord Jesus Christ. The one
who calls you is faithful and He will do it.

1 Thessalonians 5:23-24 NIV

The reward that
outdoes all others is
the peace of knowing
that you did right.

- Jack Hyles

"I have told you this so that My joy may be in you and that your joy may be complete."

John 15:11 NIV

The joy of the LORD is your strength.

Nehemiah 8:10 NIV

"Rejoice because your names
are written in heaven."

Luke 10:20 NKJV

Happy are the people whose God is the LORD!

Psalm 144:15 NKJV

A glad heart makes a happy face;
a broken heart crushes the spirit.

Proverbs 15:13 NLT

Oh, give thanks to the LORD, for He is good!
For His mercy endures forever.

Psalm 107:1 NKJV

Glory in His holy name; let the hearts
of those who seek the LORD rejoice.

1 Chronicles 16:10 NIV

Light shines on the godly, and joy
on those whose hearts are right.

Psalm 97:11 NLT

Our heart is glad in Him,
because we trust in His holy name.

Psalm 33:21 ESV

The LORD is my strength and my song;
He has given me victory.

Psalm 118:14 NLT

Those who look to him for help
will be radiant with joy; no shadow
of shame will darken their faces.

Psalm 34:5 NLT

Those who sow with tears will reap with songs
of joy. Those who go out weeping, carrying
seed to sow, will return with songs of joy,
carrying sheaves with them.

Psalm 126:5-6 NIV

The purest
joy in the world
is joy in Christ Jesus.

- Robert Murray M'Cheyne

Truly, God will not do wrong.
The Almighty will not twist justice.

Job 34:12 NLT

Let true justice prevail, so you
may live and occupy the land that
the LORD your God is giving you.

Deuteronomy 16:20 NLT

Your justice is eternal, and
Your instructions are perfectly true.

Psalm 119:142 NLT

Blessed are they who observe justice,
who do righteousness at all times!

Psalm 106:3 ESV

Great and marvelous are Your works,
O Lord God, the Almighty. Just and true
are Your ways, O King of the nations.

Revelation 15:3 NLT

He is the Lord our God.
His justice is seen throughout the land.

1 Chronicles 16:14 NLT

Lord, You always give me justice
when I bring a case before You.

Jeremiah 12:1 NLT

The righteous Lord loves justice.
The virtuous will see His face.

Psalm 11:7 NLT

The Lord will not reject His people;
He will never forsake His inheritance.
Judgment will again be founded on
righteousness, and all the upright
in heart will follow it.

Psalm 94:14-15 NIV

The Lord longs to be gracious to you; therefore He will rise up to show you compassion.
For the Lord is a God of justice. Blessed are
all who wait for Him!

Isaiah 30:18 NIV

Let God
be the Judge.
Your job today is
to be a witness.

- Warren Wiersbe

The Lord is not slow in keeping His
promise, as some understand slowness.
Instead He is patient with you.

2 Peter 3:9 NIV

The LORD is longsuffering and abundant in
mercy, forgiving iniquity and transgression.

Numbers 14:18 NKJV

Patience can persuade a prince.

Proverbs 25:15 NLT

The end of a matter is better than its
beginning, and patience is better than pride.

Ecclesiastes 7:8 NIV

I waited patiently for the LORD;
He turned to me and heard my cry.

Psalm 40:1 NIV

Remember, our Lord's patience
gives people time to be saved.

2 Peter 3:15 NLT

Better to be patient than powerful;
better to have self-control
than to conquer a city.

Proverbs 16:32 NLT

The LORD is good to those who
wait for Him, to the soul who seeks Him.

Lamentations 3:25 NKJV

Be still in the presence of the LORD,
and wait patiently for Him to act.

Psalm 37:7 NLT

Don't you see how wonderfully kind,
tolerant, and patient God is with you?

Romans 2:4 NIV

Those who wait on the LORD shall renew their
strength; they shall mount up with wings like
eagles, they shall run and not be weary,
they shall walk and not faint.

Isaiah 40:31 NKJV

Wait patiently for the LORD. Be brave and
courageous. Yes, wait patiently for the LORD.

Psalm 27:14 NLT

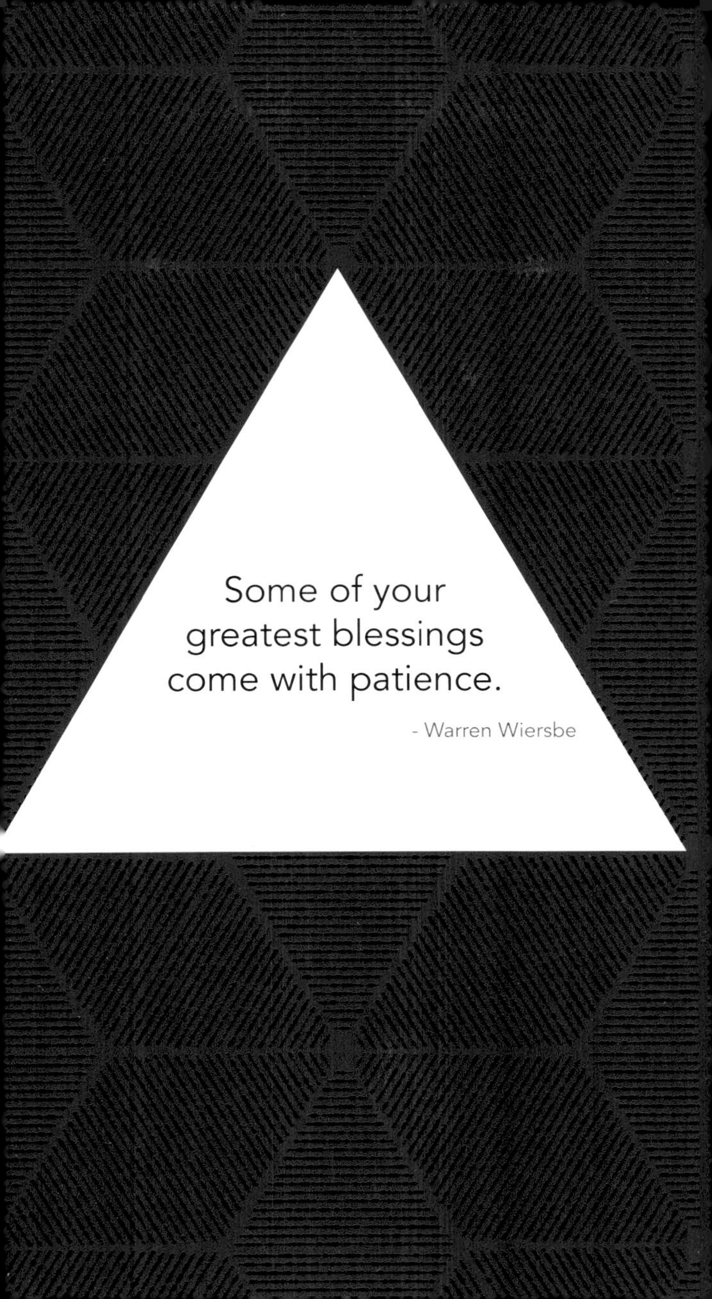

Some of your
greatest blessings
come with patience.

- Warren Wiersbe

"Peace I leave with you, My peace
I give to you; not as the world gives
do I give to you. Let not your heart
be troubled, neither let it be afraid."

John 14:27 NKJV

The peace of God, which transcends all
understanding, will guard your hearts
and your minds in Christ Jesus.

Philippians 4:7 NIV

The Lord will give strength to His people;
the Lord will bless His people with peace.

Psalm 29:11 NKJV

You will keep in perfect peace
those whose minds are steadfast,
because they trust in You.

Isaiah 26:3 NIV

May the Lord of peace Himself give you
His peace at all times and in every situation.
The Lord be with you all.

2 Thessalonians 3:16 NLT

"Come to Me, all you who labor and
are heavy laden, and I will give you rest.
Take My yoke upon you and learn from
Me, for I am gentle and lowly in heart,
and you will find rest for your souls. For
My yoke is easy and My burden is light."

Matthew 11:28-30 NKJV

There remains therefore a rest for the
people of God. For he who has entered
His rest has himself also ceased from
his works as God did from His. Let us
therefore be diligent to enter that rest.

Hebrews 4:9-11 NKJV

Mark the blameless man, and observe the
upright; for the future of that man is peace.

Psalm 37:37 NKJV

Because of God's tender mercy, the morning
light from heaven is about to break upon us,
to give light to those who sit in darkness
and in the shadow of death, and to guide
us to the path of peace.

Luke 1:78-79 NLT

As we pour
out our bitterness,
God pours in His peace.

- F. B. Meyer

The Lord – my Protector

The name of the LORD is a strong fortress;
the godly run to Him and are safe.

Proverbs 18:10 NLT

The LORD will keep you from all harm –
He will watch over your life; the LORD
will watch over your coming and going
both now and forevermore.

Psalm 121:7-8 NIV

The Lord is faithful, and He will strengthen
you and protect you from the evil one.

2 Thessalonians 3:3 NIV

"Don't be afraid, for I am with you.
Don't be discouraged, for I am your God.
I will strengthen you and help you. I will hold
you up with My victorious right hand."

Isaiah 41:10 NLT

The beloved of the LORD dwells in safety.
The High God surrounds him all day long,
and dwells between his shoulders.

Deuteronomy 33:12 ESV

When you lie down, you will not
be afraid; yes, you will lie down
and your sleep will be sweet.

Proverbs 3:24 NKJV

The LORD protects those of childlike faith.

Psalm 116:6 NLT

The LORD is my rock, my fortress, and
my Savior; my God is my rock, in whom
I find protection. He is my shield,
the power that saves me, and my place
of safety. He is my refuge, my Savior,
the one who saves me from violence.

2 Samuel 22:2-3 NLT

Blessed are those whose help is the God of
Jacob, whose hope is in the LORD their God.

Psalm 146:5 NIV

The LORD is my light and my salvation –
so why should I be afraid? The LORD is my
fortress, protecting me from danger,
so why should I tremble?

Psalm 27:1 NLT

The safest
place in all the
world is in the will
of God, and the safest
protection in all the world
is the name of God.

- Warren Wiersbe

For everything there is a season, a time
for every activity under heaven.

Ecclesiastes 3:1 NLT

Humble yourselves under the mighty hand of
God, that He may exalt you in due time.

1 Peter 5:6 NKJV

Beloved, do not forget this one thing, that
with the Lord one day is as a thousand years,
and a thousand years as one day.

2 Peter 3:8 NKJV

Before the mountains were born, before You
gave birth to the earth and the world, from
beginning to end, You are God.

Psalm 90:2 NLT

At the right time He will bring everything
together under the authority of Christ –
everything in heaven and on earth.

Ephesians 1:10 NLT

I trust in You, O Lord; I say, "You are my
God." My times are in Your hand.

Psalm 31:14-15 NKJV

Teach us to number our days,
that we may gain a heart of wisdom.

Psalm 90:12 NIV

The Lord knows the days of the blameless,
and their heritage will remain forever.

Psalm 37:18 ESV

We can make our plans, but the Lord
determines our steps.

Proverbs 16:9 NLT

Be careful how you live. Don't live like fools,
but like those who are wise. Make the most of
every opportunity in these evil days. Don't act
thoughtlessly, but understand what the Lord
wants you to do.

Ephesians 5:15-17 NLT

The surest
method of arriving
at a knowledge of
God's eternal purposes
about us is to be found in the
right use of the present moment.

- Frederick W. Faber

Trust in the LORD with all your heart;
do not depend on your own understanding.
Seek His will in all you do, and He will
show you which path to take.

Proverbs 3:5-6 NLT

Blessed is that man who makes
the LORD his trust.

Psalm 40:4 NKJV

Trust in Him at all times; pour out your heart
before Him; God is a refuge for us.

Psalm 62:8 NKJV

The LORD is good, a refuge in times of trouble.
He cares for those who trust in Him.

Nahum 1:7 NIV

Trust in the LORD always, for
the LORD GOD is the eternal Rock.

Isaiah 26:4 NLT

"I am the LORD, and I do not change."

Malachi 3:6 NLT

Every good and perfect gift is from above,
coming down from the Father of the
heavenly lights, who does not change
like shifting shadows.

James 1:17 NIV

Let the morning bring me word of
Your unfailing love, for I have put
my trust in You.

Psalm 143:8 NIV

In God I have put my trust; I will not be afraid.
What can man do to me?

Psalm 56:11 NKJV

The Scriptures tell us, "Anyone who
trusts in Him will never be disgraced."

Romans 10:11 NLT

Trust in Him at all times, you people; pour out
your hearts to Him, for God is our refuge.

Psalm 62:8 NIV

Nothing
is too great
and nothing is
too small to commit
into the hands of the Lord.

- A. W. Pink

Jesus said; "You will know the truth,
and the truth will set you free."

John 8:32 NLT

Lead me in Your truth and teach me,
for You are the God of my salvation;
on You I wait all the day.

Psalm 25:5 NKJV

The LORD is near to all who call upon Him,
to all who call upon Him in truth.

Psalm 145:18 NKJV

The LORD detests lying lips, but
He delights in those who tell the truth.

Proverbs 12:22 NLT

Jesus said, "I am the way, the truth,
and the life. No one comes to
the Father except through Me."

John 14:6 NKJV

His merciful kindness is great toward us,
and the truth of the Lord endures forever.
Praise the Lord!

Psalm 117:2 NKJV

He shall cover you with His feathers, and
under His wings you shall take refuge;
His truth shall be your shield and buckler.

Psalm 91:4 NKJV

The Lord is good; His mercy is everlasting,
and His truth endures to all generations.

Psalm 100:5 NKJV

When the Spirit of truth comes,
He will guide you into all truth.

John 16:13 NLT

God is not a man, so He does not lie. He is
not human, so He does not change His mind.
Has He ever spoken and failed to act? Has He
ever promised and not carried it through?

Numbers 23:19 NLT

Truth is not
what I say it is,
and not what you
think it is. Truth is what
God's Word says it is.

- John Hagee

If any of you lacks wisdom, you should ask
God, who gives generously to all without
finding fault, and it will be given to you.

James 1:5 NIV

With Him are wisdom and strength,
He has counsel and understanding.

Job 12:13 NKJV

The wisdom that is from above is first pure,
then peaceable, gentle, willing to yield,
full of mercy and good fruits, without
partiality and without hypocrisy.

James 3:17 NKJV

Joyful is the person who finds wisdom,
the one who gains understanding.

Proverbs 3:13 NLT

Your commands make me wiser than my
enemies, for they are my constant guide.

Psalm 119:98 NLT

The LORD gives wisdom; from His mouth
come knowledge and understanding.

Proverbs 2:6 NKJV

My goal is that they may be encouraged
in heart and united in love, so that they
may have the full riches of complete
understanding, in order that they may
know the mystery of God, namely, Christ,
in whom are hidden all the treasures
of wisdom and knowledge.

Colossians 2:2-3 NIV

The foolishness of God is wiser than human
wisdom, and the weakness of God is stronger
than human strength.

1 Corinthians 1:25 NIV

Teach us to realize the brevity of life,
so that we may grow in wisdom.

Psalm 90:12 NLT

If you lack
knowledge,
go to school. If
you lack wisdom, get
on your knees! Knowledge
is not wisdom. Wisdom is
the proper use of knowledge.

- Vance Havner

If our hearts condemn us, we know that
God is greater than our hearts,
and He knows everything.

1 John 3:20 NIV

Do not be afraid or discouraged, for
the LORD will personally go ahead of you.
He will be with you; He will neither
fail you nor abandon you.

Deuteronomy 31:8 NLT

Though I am surrounded by troubles,
You will protect me from the anger of my
enemies. You reach out Your hand, and the
power of Your right hand saves me.

Psalm 138:7 NLT

When the cares of my heart are many,
Your consolations cheer my soul.

Psalm 94:19 ESV

Cast your cares on the LORD and He
will sustain you; He will never let
the righteous be shaken.

Psalm 55:22 NIV

God has not given us a spirit of fear, but of
power and of love and of a sound mind.

2 Timothy 1:7 NKJV

Give all your worries and cares to God,
for He cares about you.

1 Peter 5:7 NLT

In righteousness you shall be established;
you shall be far from oppression, for
you shall not fear; and from terror,
for it shall not come near you.

Isaiah 54:14 NKJV

God will wipe away every tear from their eyes;
there shall be no more death, nor sorrow,
nor crying. There shall be no more pain,
for the former things have passed away.

Revelation 21:4 NKJV

I know the LORD is always with me. I will not
be shaken, for He is right beside me.

Psalm 16:8 NLT

Worry does not
empty tomorrow
of its sorrow. It empties
today of its strength.

- Corrie ten Boom

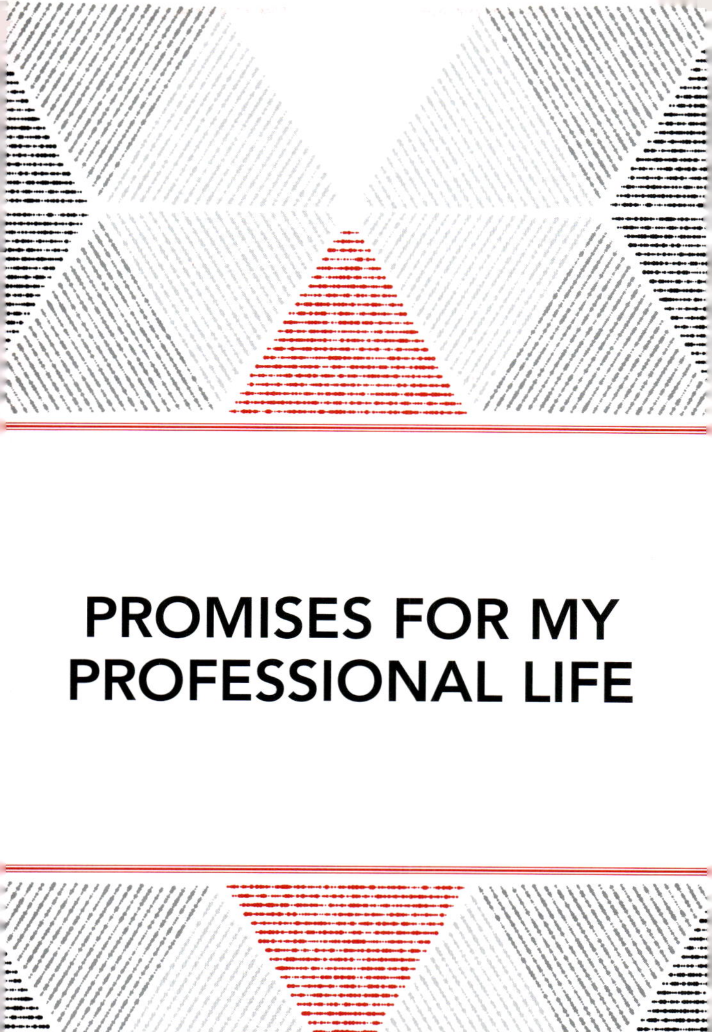

PROMISES FOR MY PROFESSIONAL LIFE

Stand firm. Let nothing move you.
Always give yourselves fully to the work
of the Lord, because you know that your
labor in the Lord is not in vain.

1 Corinthians 15:58 NIV

Be all the more diligent to confirm your
calling and election, for if you practice
these qualities you will never fall.

2 Peter 1:10 ESV

May He grant your heart's desires and
make all your plans succeed.

Psalm 20:4 NLT

Pay careful attention to your own work,
for then you will get the satisfaction of
a job well done, and you won't need to
compare yourself to anyone else.

Galatians 6:4 NLT

The LORD will send rain at the proper time
from His rich treasury in the heavens and
will bless all the work you do.

Deuteronomy 28:12 NLT

Be strong and do not let your hands be weak,
for your work shall be rewarded!

2 Chronicles 15:7 NKJV

The Lord says, "I will guide you along
the best pathway for your life. I will
advise you and watch over you."

Psalm 32:8 NLT

Commit your work to the LORD,
and your plans will be established.

Proverbs 16:3 ESV

Work willingly at whatever you do,
as though you were working for
the Lord rather than for people.
Remember that the Lord will give
you an inheritance as your reward.

Colossians 3:23-24 NLT

Make it your goal to live a quiet life, minding
your own business and working with your
hands. Then people who are not believers
will respect the way you live, and you will
not need to depend on others.

1 Thessalonians 4:11-12 NLT

Faithful servants
never retire. You can
retire from your career,
but you will never
retire from serving God.

- Rick Warren

The LORD will make you abound in prosperity,
in the fruit of your womb and in the fruit
of your livestock and in the fruit of your
ground, within the land that the LORD
swore to your fathers to give you.

Deuteronomy 28:11 ESV

You will succeed in whatever you
choose to do, and light will shine
on the road ahead of you.

Job 22:28 NLT

Take delight in the LORD, and He will
give you the desires of your heart.

Psalm 37:4 NIV

The desire of the righteous
ends only in good.

Proverbs 11:23 NIV

Jesus said, "With man this is impossible,
but with God all things are possible."

Matthew 19:26 NIV

A generous person will prosper; whoever
refreshes others will be refreshed.

Proverbs 11:25 NIV

Remember the LORD your God. He is the one
who gives you power to be successful.

Deuteronomy 8:18 NLT

All glory to God, who is able, through His
mighty power at work within us, to accomplish
infinitely more than we might ask or think.

Ephesians 3:20 NLT

May the Lord our God show us His
approval and make our efforts successful.
Yes, make our efforts successful!

Psalm 90:17 NLT

May God give you the power to
accomplish all the good things
your faith prompts you to do.

2 Thessalonians 1:11 NLT

You, LORD, have made me glad
through Your work; I will triumph
in the works of Your hands.

Psalm 92:4 NKJV

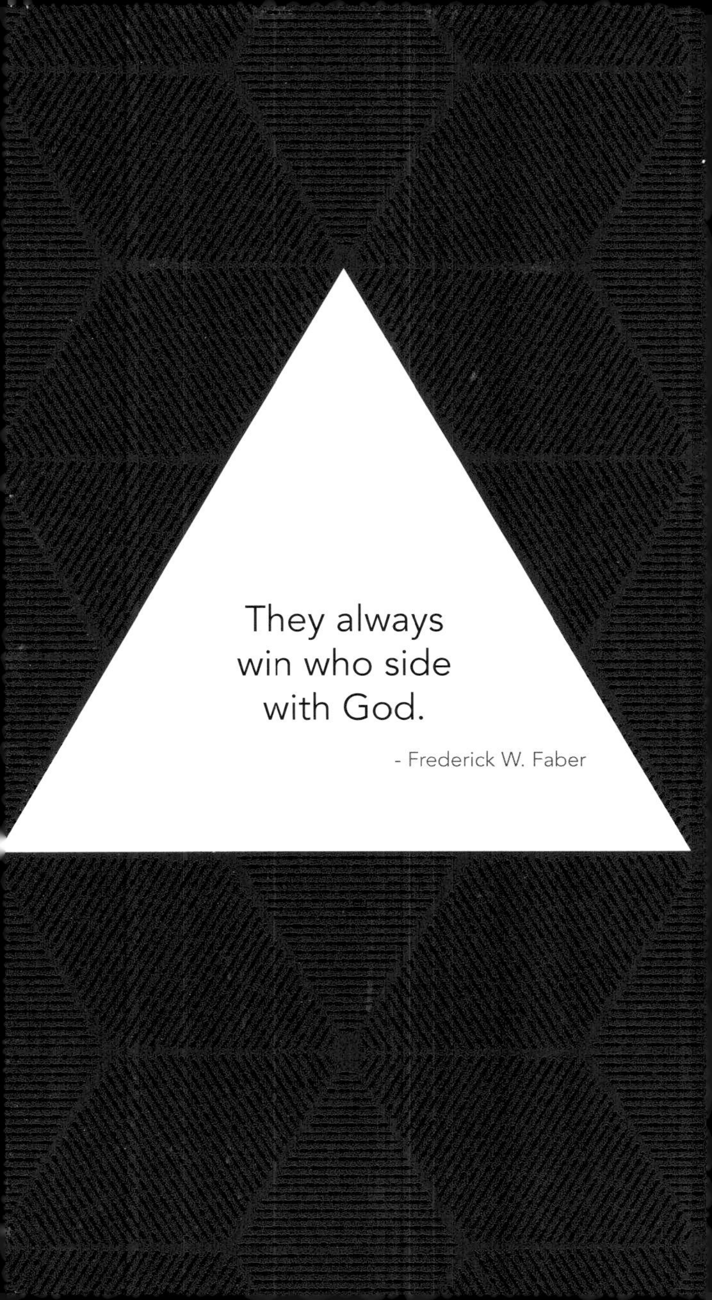

They always
win who side
with God.

- Frederick W. Faber

Whatever you do, do it heartily,
as to the Lord and not to men,
knowing that from the Lord you will
receive the reward of the inheritance.

Colossians 3:23-24 NKJV

"Be strong, all you people of the land,"
declares the LORD, "and work. For I am
with you," declares the LORD Almighty.

Haggai 2:4 NIV

The LORD your God will bless you in all
your harvest and in all the work of your
hands, and your joy will be complete.

Deuteronomy 16:15 NIV

You shall eat the fruit of the labor
of your hands; you shall be blessed,
and it shall be well with you.

Psalm 128:2 ESV

All hard work brings a profit,
but mere talk leads only to poverty.

Proverbs 14:23 NIV

Anyone who enters God's rest also rests from
their works, just as God did from His.

Hebrews 4:10 NIV

It is a good thing to receive wealth
from God and the good health to enjoy it.
To enjoy your work and accept your lot
in life – this is indeed a gift from God.

Ecclesiastes 5:19 NLT

The one who plants and the one who waters
work together with the same purpose. And
both will be rewarded for their own hard work.

1 Corinthians 3:8 NLT

God is not unjust. He will not forget
how hard you have worked for Him and
how you have shown your love to Him
by caring for other believers.

Hebrews 6:10 NLT

It is in vain that you rise up early and go
late to rest, eating the bread of anxious toil;
for He gives to His beloved sleep.

Psalm 127:2 ESV

If God called
us to a task,
He will then qualify
us for the job.

- Jack Hyles

PROMISES OF A NEW LIFE

Salvation is for everyone

Truly my soul finds rest in God;
my salvation comes from Him.
Truly He is my rock and my salvation;
He is my fortress, I will never be shaken.

Psalm 62:1-2 NIV

God is my King from long ago;
He brings salvation on the earth.

Psalm 74:12 NIV

"It is I, the LORD, announcing your salvation!
It is I, the LORD, who has the power to save!"

Isaiah 63:1 NLT

"Call on Me when you are in trouble, and I
will rescue you, and you will give Me glory."

Psalm 50:15 NLT

God did not appoint us to suffer wrath
but to receive salvation through
our Lord Jesus Christ.

1 Thessalonians 5:9 NIV

Christ, having been offered once to bear
the sins of many, will appear a second time,
not to deal with sin, but to save those who are
eagerly waiting for Him.

Hebrews 9:28 ESV

"God did not send His Son into the world
to condemn the world, but that the world
through Him might be saved. He who
believes in Him is not condemned."

John 3:17-18 NKJV

Everyone who calls on the name
of the Lord will be saved.

Romans 10:13 NV

"I have come that they may have life,
and have it to the full."

John 10:10 NIV

Behold, God is my salvation; I will trust,
and will not be afraid; for the LORD GOD
is my strength and my song, and He
has become my salvation.

Isaiah 12:2 ESV

Salvation
comes through
a cross and a
crucified Christ.

- Andrew Murray

If anyone is in Christ, the new creation has come: The old has gone, the new is here!

2 Corinthians 5:17 NIV

Put on your new nature, and be renewed as you learn to know your Creator and become like Him.

Colossians 3:10 NLT

He saved us, not because of the righteous things we had done, but because of His mercy. He washed away our sins, giving us a new birth and new life through the Holy Spirit. He generously poured out the Spirit upon us through Jesus Christ our Savior.

Titus 3:5-6 NLT

Don't copy the behavior and customs of this world, but let God transform you into a new person by changing the way you think. Then you will learn to know God's will for you, which is good and pleasing and perfect.

Romans 12:2 NLT

You were buried with Christ when you were baptized. And with Him you were raised to new life because you trusted the mighty power of God, who raised Christ from the dead.

Colossians 2:12 NLT

Give yourselves completely to God, for you were dead, but now you have new life. So use your whole body as an instrument to do what is right for the glory of God. Sin is no longer your master, for you no longer live under the requirements of the law. Instead, you live under the freedom of God's grace.

Romans 6:13-14 NLT

You were taught, with regard to your former way of life, to put off your old self, which is being corrupted by its deceitful desires; to be made new in the attitude of your minds; and to put on the new self, created to be like God in true righteousness and holiness.

Ephesians 4:22-24 NIV

Revival
begins in the
individual's heart.
Let it begin with you
on your face alone before
God. Turn from every sin that
might hinder. Renew yourself to
a new devotion to the Savior.

- Lee Roberson

"Don't let your hearts be troubled. Trust in God, and trust also in Me. There is more than enough room in My Father's home. If this were not so, would I have told you that I am going to prepare a place for you? When everything is ready, I will come and get you, so that you will always be with Me where I am."

John 14:1-3 NLT

"Don't store up treasures here on earth, where moths eat them and rust destroys them, and where thieves break in and steal. Store your treasures in heaven, where moths and rust cannot destroy, and thieves do not break in and steal. Wherever your treasure is, there the desires of your heart will also be."

Matthew 6:19-21 NLT

"My sheep listen to My voice; I know them, and they follow Me. I give them eternal life, and they shall never perish; no one will snatch them out of My hand."

John 10:27-28 NIV

The free gift of God is eternal life
in Christ Jesus our Lord.

Romans 6:23 ESV

God showed how much He loved us by
sending His one and only Son into the
world so that we might have
eternal life through Him.

1 John 4:9 NLT

"God so loved the world, that He gave
His only Son, that whoever believes in Him
should not perish but have eternal life."

John 3:16 ESV

"My Father's will is that everyone who
looks to the Son and believes in Him
shall have eternal life, and I will raise
them up at the last day."

John 6:40 NIV

"Those who have done good
will rise to experience eternal life."

John 5:29 NLT

The best
moment of a
Christian's life is
his last one, because
it is the one that is
nearest heaven. And then
it is that he begins to strike
the keynote of the song which
he shall sing to all eternity.

- Charles H. Spurgeon